Smithsonian

Exploring
the
Georgia
Colony

by Brianna Hall

CAPSTONE PRESS
a capstone imprint

Smithsonian books are published by Capstone Press,
1710 Roe Crest Drive, North Mankato, Minnesota 56003
www.capstonepub.com

The name of the Smithsonian Institution and the sunburst logo are registered trademarks of the
Smithsonian Institution. For more information, please visit www.si.edu.

Library of Congress Cataloging-in-Publication Data
Names: Hall, Brianna, author.
Title: Exploring the Georgia Colony / by Brianna Hall.
Description: North Mankato, Minnesota: Capstone Press, [2017] | Series:
    Smithsonian. Exploring the 13 colonies. | Includes bibliographical
    references and index. | Summary: "This book explores the people, places,
    and history of the Georgia Colony"— Provided by publisher. | Audience:
    Ages 8–11.
Identifiers: LCCN 2016013023| ISBN 9781515722410 (library binding: alk.
    paper) | ISBN 9781515722540 (pbk.: alk. paper) | ISBN 9781515722670
    (ebook: .pdf)
Subjects: LCSH: Georgia—History—Colonial period, ca. 1600–1775—Juvenile
    literature.
Classification: LCC F289 .H18 2017 | DDC 975.8/02—dc23
LC record available at http://lccn.loc.gov/2016013023

Editorial Credits
Gina Kammer, editor; Richard Parker, designer; Eric Gohl, media researcher;
Kathy McColley, production specialist

Our very special thanks to Stephen Binns at the Smithsonian Center for Learning and Digital Access for
his curatorial review. Capstone would also like to thank Kealy Gordon, Smithsonian Institution Product
Development Manager, and the following at Smithsonian Enterprises: Christopher A. Liedel, President;
Carol LeBlanc, Senior Vice President; Brigid Ferraro, Vice President; Ellen Nanney, Licensing Manager.

Photo Credits
Alamy: Everett Collection Historical, 36, George H.H. Huey, 19; Bridgeman Images: Peter Newark
Pictures/Private Collection, 32; Capstone: 4; Courtesy of the Georgia Historical Society: 33; Courtesy
of Hargrett Rare Book and Manuscript Library/University of Georgia Libraries: 6; Georgia Archives:
16; Getty Images: Hulton Archive, 22, 25, Kean Collection, 34, Stringer/MPI, 20; Granger, NYC: cover,
7, 9, 17, 26, 27, 38; Library of Congress: 12; New York Public Library: 10, 14, 39, 41 (all); North Wind
Picture Archives: 8, 11, 13, 18, 24, 28, 29, 30, 35, 37; SuperStock: 31; Wikimedia: Jud McCranie, 23, Public
Domain, 15, 21, 40

Design Elements: Shutterstock

Printed and bound in the USA.
009669F16

Table of Contents

Introduction:
The 13 Colonies

In 1492 Christopher Columbus arrived in America and opened a "New World" for Europeans. The Spanish would come in search of gold. The French would begin a fur trade with Native Americans. The English would eventually establish 13 **Colonies** on the eastern coast of North America. Colonies are lands controlled by a faraway country. People left their homes in England for better opportunities in the colonies. Some wanted religious freedom or their own land to farm. Others just wanted a new way of life.

Settlers arrived in the first colony, Virginia, in 1607. Georgia, named for King George II, was not settled until more than a hundred years later in 1733. Georgia was the last of the 13 Colonies to be founded. All colonists faced similar hardships in starting their lives over again in a new land. The first colonists had to build shelter, learn to find and grow food, and get used to new climates and landscapes.

Georgia was in the Southern Colonies region. It was the most southern of the 13 Colonies.

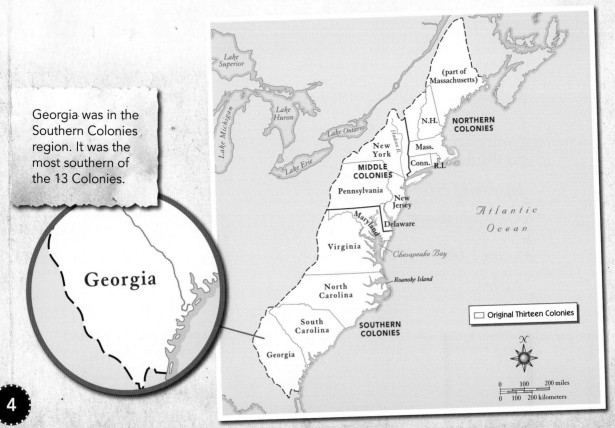

The Original 13 Colonies

The first permanent European settlement in each colony:

Virginia	1607	Delaware	1638
Massachusetts	1620	Pennsylvania	1643
New Hampshire	1623	North Carolina	1653
New York	1624	New Jersey	1660
Connecticut	1633	South Carolina	1670
Maryland	1634	Georgia	1733
Rhode Island	1636		

England controlled the 13 Colonies, so the settlers were still subject to England's laws, even though they lived across the ocean. The colonies began as tiny villages, but they grew. In the Northern Colonies, such as Massachusetts, villages became bustling cities with factories, schools, and banks. Along the southern coast in colonies such as South Carolina and Georgia, most colonists lived on farms. Although northern colonists and southern colonists disagreed about many things, they shared a desire for independence from England's control.

As the last English colony established in America, Georgia was different from the other 12. It did not have its own government. Instead a group of Englishmen called **trustees** made all the decisions. Eventually Georgia's colonists broke free from the trustees. And after 43 years as colonists, they fought to break free from England too.

colony—a place that is settled by people from another country and is controlled by that country

trustee—a person who has been given responsibility for someone else's property

Chapter 1:
Native Nations

Native Americans called the area of Georgia home for thousands of years before Europeans arrived. The powerful Cherokee nation lived in northwestern Georgia, while the smaller Yamasee and Hitchiti tribes lived in the south. The Yamacraw and Creek nations lived in the central and coastal regions.

Cherokees

The word "Cherokee" comes from the Creek language and means "people of different speech." A large and powerful nation, the Cherokees built tall fences around their towns to keep enemies out. They mainly lived in rectangular cabins but used smaller, dome-shaped houses in winter because they were easier to keep warm.

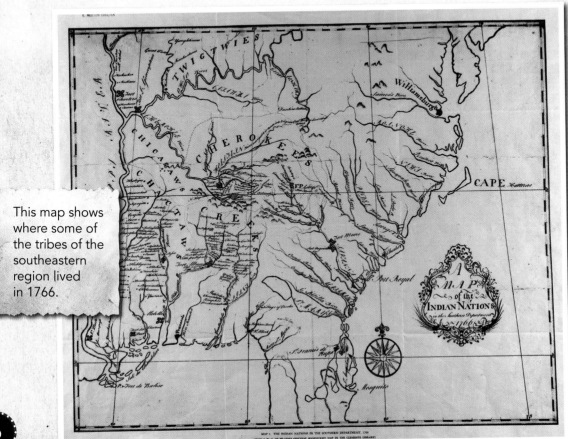

This map shows where some of the tribes of the southeastern region lived in 1766.

Creeks

The Creek **Confederacy** thrived along the banks of Georgia's rivers. Its population in 1733 was approximately 10,000 people. These people were spread out over 35 towns throughout America's southeastern region. Each town had a leader who persuaded townspeople to follow the laws. Each town centered around a public square with religious and political buildings.

The Town Creek Indian Mound site shows examples of southern Native American homes before Colonial times, including religious structures.

According to Creek culture, men, women, and children had very specific jobs. Men hunted and fought battles. Women were in charge of the land, planting and harvesting corn and squash. Children played games like toli, a sport similar to lacrosse, on the public ball field.

There were also smaller groups of Native Americans. The Yamacraws were a mixed group of Creeks and Yamasees who left their homes to start new lives. A Creek town had **banished** a man named Tomochichi, so he started the Yamacraw group and became its leader. In 1728 he established a new community on Yamacraw Bluff along the Savannah River.

The arrival of Europeans changed the ways of life for Georgia's native people. Europeans brought not only a new religion and new customs to America but also diseases that killed many Native Americans. The Native Americans also fought with Spain and France for land.

Chief Tomochichi (1644?–1739)

Tomochichi grew up in the Lower Creek town of Apalachicola learning hunting and riding like other Creek boys. As a young man, he became a warrior and businessman. Tomochichi traded goods and Native American slaves. The Creek Confederacy banished Tomochichi, but historians do not know why. He then started the Yamacraw group.

When English colonists first settled near Yamacraw Bluff, Chief Tomochichi became an important **diplomat** between the Creeks and the settlers. In 1734 he sailed across the Atlantic Ocean to London, England. He discussed trade agreements and education with King George II and the trustees. Tomochichi's decisions and leadership helped establish peace between the colonists and Native Americans.

Critical Thinking with Primary Sources

This painting shows Georgia's trustees meeting with some members of the Creek tribe in London. What does this painting tell you about England in 1734? Compare the Englishmen's clothing to the Creeks' clothing. James Oglethorpe, the founder of the Georgia Colony, is the man wearing black in the center of the painting. He is holding hands with a Creek child dressed in English clothing. What do you think this symbolizes?

banish—to force someone to leave a country as a punishment

diplomat—someone who deals with other nations to create or maintain good relationships

Chapter 2:
The Race for Georgia

The struggle to control Georgia was like a global game of tug-of-war among the Native Americans, Spanish, English, and French. Sometimes the players talked to each other and reached agreements. Other times they went to war.

Spanish Exploration

Europeans did not explore the Georgia area until 1526 when Spanish settlers tried, and failed, to set up colonies on the land. Spanish military leader Hernando de Soto and 600 soldiers crossed into Georgia from Florida in 1540. Though in search of gold, they captured and enslaved hundreds of Creeks and other native people. They also killed thousands in battle. De Soto and half of his crew died from disease, starvation, or warfare on their journey across the South.

Hernando de Soto explored much of southern North America.

"... a hundred men and women were taken ... They were led off in chains, with collars about the neck, to carry luggage and grind corn, doing the labor proper to servants ..."

—The Gentleman of Elvas, an unnamed soldier in de Soto's raiding party

Hernando de Soto forced Native Americans to be his guides or work for him.

In the 1560s the Spanish built Catholic **missions** along the Georgia coast. Soldiers and Catholic religious leaders lived at the missions. However, Spanish settlement hurt native populations. The Spanish at the missions carried European diseases such as smallpox, which spread quickly and caused fevers and scarring pimples. The Native Americans had no defenses against these diseases, so many of them died.

Europeans Nations Clash

At the same time, England and France established relationships with the Creeks. And about a century later, the English wanted to protect their newest colony, South Carolina. They formed military **alliances** with the Native Americans. The French wanted to extend their trade network from the Mississippi River to the Atlantic Coast. They traded animal furs and deerskin.

Spain sent Pedro Menendez de Aviles to Florida to establish a colony in 1565. Later, he and his soldiers built 38 missions.

French traders, Creek warriors, English travelers, and Spanish soldiers clashed. Traveling became dangerous as the four groups fought to control the land. Even townspeople and farmers lived in fear of attack. Settlers on the frontier of the South Carolina Colony asked King George II for protection from the fighting.

South Carolina colonists fought with Creeks on the Georgia frontier.

mission—a church or other place where people from a religious group live and work trying to spread their faith

alliance—an agreement between groups to work together

Chapter 3:
A Place for England's Poor

The Georgia Trustees proposed a new colony. It would both protect South Carolina from the Spanish and give hope to the poor of England. At the time thousands of people were moving from England's countryside to its cities, but they could not find work. If poor people could not pay their debts, they were put into cruel **debtors**' prisons. The trustees, led by James Oglethorpe, thought they could help the poor start over in the colony of Georgia.

James Edward Oglethorpe (1696–1784)

Born in London, James Oglethorpe grew up in a wealthy family. He served in the British Army before becoming a member of **Parliament**. Oglethorpe gave his money away to worthy causes. He felt that helping the poor was one of these causes. In his lifetime people celebrated his leadership. He is called "the Father of Georgia."

The Georgia Colony became his life's work. As the only trustee living in Georgia, Oglethorpe made most decisions for the colony. He worked alongside the colonists, made agreements with Native Americans, and sailed between England and Georgia several times. He was a hardworking and forward-thinking leader.

Oglethorpe's Plan

Oglethorpe and a group of 20 English trustees wrote a proposal for the Georgia Colony in 1730. It contained many rules, but it put an importance on fairness. The plan called for the trustees to pay for poor peoples' boat passage to America. Once in America every poor male settler of Georgia would receive 50 acres of land. Settlers who paid their own way could own up to 500 acres. As part of the plan, the trustees also provided farming supplies for every colonist. In exchange settlers had to live and work in Georgia for at least three years. The plan was to establish small towns instead of big cities because the trustees believed that cities caused poverty. Oglethorpe imagined orderly towns with public squares.

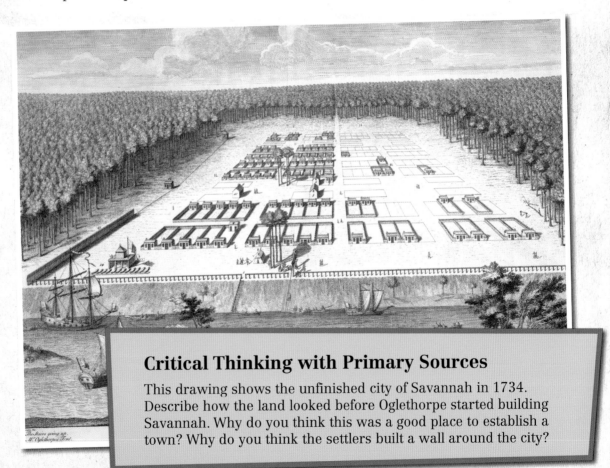

Critical Thinking with Primary Sources

This drawing shows the unfinished city of Savannah in 1734. Describe how the land looked before Oglethorpe started building Savannah. Why do you think this was a good place to establish a town? Why do you think the settlers built a wall around the city?

debtor—someone who owes money to another person or organization
Parliament—Great Britain's lawmaking body

Oglethorpe's plan also outlawed the sale of Africans as slaves. This set Georgia apart from the other colonies. However, owning Native American slaves and **indentured servants** was legal.

The Georgia Experiment Begins

In June 1732 King George II approved the colony of Georgia with a royal **charter**. The charter allowed the colony to be run by trustees until 1753, when it would become a **royal colony**. It also set up rights for Georgia's colonists. Although the charter granted Georgia's colonists religious freedom, it outlawed Catholicism to upset Britain's rivals in the Catholic nation of Spain.

The trustees wrote persuasive articles to raise money for their experiment. Their motto was "not for self, but for others." Wealthy families donated money and supplies.

Oglethorpe assembled a group of families, artisans, and soldiers. On November 17, 1732, 114 people sailed for Georgia aboard a ship named the *Ann*. They arrived three months later, on February 12, 1733. The colonists established the town of Savannah at Yamacraw Bluff on the Savannah River.

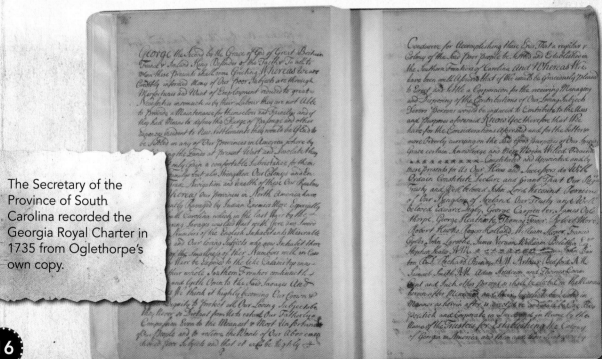

The Secretary of the Province of South Carolina recorded the Georgia Royal Charter in 1735 from Oglethorpe's own copy.

> *"... there shall be a liberty of conscience allowed in the worship of God ... all persons ... except papists [Catholics], shall have a free exercise of their religion ..."*
>
> —From the Royal Charter of 1732

Georgia's first settlers cut down trees to build houses and other buildings in Savannah.

Did You Know?

Georgia's citizens celebrate Georgia Day each year on February 12.

indentured servant—a person who works for someone else for a certain period of time in return for payment of travel and living costs

charter—an official document granting permission to set up a new colony, organization, or company

royal colony—a colony controlled by a monarch or his representatives

Building the Colony

The colonists got to work building homes and shops. Some of the first buildings erected included a guardhouse, a courthouse, and a mill. Oglethorpe worked alongside the colonists. He acted as judge and doctor. He served on guard duty, worked as head architect, and helped during construction.

Chief Tomochichi met with Oglethorpe shortly after the *Ann* arrived. Mary Musgrove, a woman who was half-Creek with an English father translated for Tomochichi and Oglethorpe. It took some time, but the Yamacraws agreed to give land to the settlers to establish the town of Savannah. As a sign of goodwill, Tomochichi gave "white wings of peace" to the colonists. They looked like large, elaborate fans of white feathers. In response Oglethorpe presented Tomochichi with gifts from England.

Tomochichi and Oglethorpe shake hands as a sign of their friendship.

Mary Musgrove (1700?–1764?)

With a Creek mother and English father, Mary Musgrove lived a life between two cultures. She was born around 1700 in the Creek village of Coweta. As a girl and teenager, Mary lived in South Carolina with her father. In 1732 she and her husband moved to the frontier near Yamacraw Bluff.

Women rarely worked in politics in Colonial America, but Musgrove became an interpreter and diplomat. She spoke English and the Creek language of Muskogee, which allowed her to translate for Oglethorpe and Tomochichi. She helped keep peace during Georgia's early years and brought the Creeks and English together during the War of Jenkins' Ear.

Mary asked the governments of Georgia and London for fair pay in exchange for her work. They promised her land but did not give it to her. She continued to fight, and in 1760 they gave her St. Catherines Island off the coast of Georgia as payment for her services.

About half of St. Catherines Island is marsh and wetlands. The island's white, sandy beach extends nearly 11 miles down Georgia's coast.

Chapter 4:
A New Colony

The Georgia Colony began as a place for England's poor, but other European **immigrants** settled there too. Some came for religious freedom. King George II offered a place in Georgia for a group of German-speaking **Protestants** who fled their Catholic government. They arrived from Salzburg (in present-day Austria) in 1734.

A group of Jewish settlers arrived in Savannah in 1733, just five months after the colony was founded. Forty Quaker families moved to Georgia from North Carolina in 1768. The royal governor gave the group 12,000 acres of land because he wanted to encourage people from other colonies to settle in Georgia. The Quakers who came to farm the land believed slavery was wrong. They did not purchase slaves to grow their tobacco and cotton. Other immigrants from Scotland, Ireland, Wales, and Holland came for new business opportunities. As a result Georgia's immigrant population did not have as many English poor as Oglethorpe had hoped.

Tobacco was shipped to other countries from the American Colonies.

During Georgia's early years, the colonists lived in peace with the Yamacraws. However, to the south, Spain was still a threat. Oglethorpe knew his colony was in danger, so he sailed back to England in 1734 to ask for help. Oglethorpe needed money to build forts to defend Georgia from the Spanish. King George II granted him the money.

King George II helped Oglethorpe by giving him money.

Did You Know?

The trustees wanted to establish a silk industry in Georgia. They even consulted Italian silk masters for advice. Unfortunately Georgia's late frosts killed the silkworms, and the experiment failed.

immigrant—someone who comes from one country to live permanently in another country

Protestant—a Christian who does not belong to the Roman Catholic or the Orthodox Church

The War of Jenkins' Ear

After Oglethorpe returned to Georgia, violence between the Spanish and colonists increased. Spanish ships started raiding English ships off the coast of Georgia. Then Spain's Native American allies began attacking colonists' farms in Georgia. In 1736 Oglethorpe sailed to England again. This time the king named him Georgia's sole military leader, and Oglethorpe sailed back with 600 soldiers. Britain declared war on the Spanish on October 23, 1739. The war became known as the War of Jenkins' Ear, which was part of a series of wars between European countries.

Robert Jenkins shows his cut-off ear to a member of Parliament.

The War of Jenkins' Ear dragged on for years. Mary Musgrove helped recruit Creek soldiers for Oglethorpe's army. Colonists from South Carolina and Georgia joined the army too. Even so they totaled less than 1,000 soldiers. The Spanish did not send all of their 5,000 troops to meet Oglethorpe, but they still outnumbered Oglethorpe's troops. Oglethorpe tried a bold new plan on July 7, 1742. His troops hid in the bushes and made a surprise attack. It worked. The fight became known as the Battle of Bloody Marsh. The colonists' style of fighting, known as **guerrilla warfare**, came in handy against the British during the Revolutionary War (1775–1783).

The site where the Battle of Bloody Marsh took place is now a quiet, peaceful place.

smuggler—a person who sneaks illegal goods into or out of a country

guerrilla warfare—a battle strategy using small groups of fighters to carry out surprise attacks against enemy forces

A Failed Experiment

The victory at Bloody Marsh helped end the War of Jenkins' Ear, but it did little to stop Oglethorpe's troubles. The Georgia Colony was not thriving. The colonists tried to grow crops there, but many had never farmed before. The plants died in Georgia's long, hot summers. Strict rules about owning land also made it difficult for people to make money. Georgia's colonists felt jealous of the other 12 colonies. They noticed that their neighbor South Carolina grew crops on large, successful plantations. Slave labor made such large farms possible.

Georgian settlers struggled to farm their land. Many wanted to use slaves to work for them, but slavery wasn't allowed in Georgia.

Kidnapped people from Africa were brought to America on crowded ships to become slaves. Oglethorpe, however, did not want Georgia to use slaves.

A political group called the malcontents wrote a protest to the trustees in 1738. Their letter called for legalized slavery, fewer rules when buying land, and representatives in the government. Oglethorpe denied them, but later the trustees slowly gave in to many of their demands.

As Georgia's population shrank, Great Britain was losing money on the colony. In 1742 the king decided to stop funding it, which forced the trustees to make changes. The group made slavery legal in 1751 and changed land-owning laws. Slave traders captured African slaves from the Caribbean Islands to sell in Georgia. Oglethorpe, who had returned to England in 1743, felt betrayed. He quit the trustees and never returned to Georgia.

Chapter 5:
Life in the King's Colony

In 1752 the trustees gave up their charter to the British government a year early. Georgia then became a royal colony like other American Colonies. This meant the king appointed a governor, and colonists had more power in government. However, the government did not include women, African-Americans, Native Americans, or people who did not own land.

Even so Georgia grew under royal leadership. New families moved to Georgia from Virginia and the Carolinas. Plantations along the Atlantic coast became bigger, and Savannah boomed with skilled workers such as blacksmiths, **seamstresses**, and tailors. The British signed treaties with the Creeks to gain more land. New settlers started farms. Between 1750 and 1773, the population grew from 5,000 to 33,000 people. But nearly half of those people were enslaved men, women, and children.

Plantation owners lived in large houses on their tobacco or rice farms.

Slaves often lived in small shacks on the plantations where they were forced to work.

Starting in 1766 the enslaved people in Georgia included people from West Africa. Whether children or adults, slaves were considered plantation owners' property. They did not live freely. During the day slave drivers forced them to labor in **indigo** and rice fields. Other slaves were forced to cook, clean, and wash clothes. At night slaves slept in shacks on the plantation. Children of adult slaves became slaves when they were born, and they usually lived as slaves their entire lives.

seamstress—a woman who sews for a living
indigo—a plant that produces a deep-blue dye

Daily Life

The majority of Georgia's citizens did not have very much money. They became known as "uplanders" because they lived on small farms away from the coast. Wooden farmhouses typically had one level. The whole family shared two or three rooms. Women on these farms grew large gardens to feed their families all year. They spun cotton and wool into thread, which they wove to make clothes. Men planted crops such as wheat and corn. Some grew tobacco or cotton to sell in town and throughout the colonies. Farming families raised cows, pigs, and horses.

The people of Georgia experienced hot, muggy summers. Mosquitoes thrived in the still water of the swamps and rice fields. Their buzz filled the air. Mosquito bites spread malaria and yellow fever. These diseases caused chills, fevers, and other serious health problems. Georgians came to call summer the "sick season" because so many people fell ill.

Uplander families kept much smaller farms than plantation owners.

Education and Trade

In Colonial Georgia schools were rare in rural areas. Typically boys and girls attended just long enough to learn how to read and write. They walked long distances to get to school, braving wild animals on the way.

Children in towns were more likely to attend school, but there were not enough public schools for everyone. Private schools popped up in Savannah. Wealthy plantation owners sent their children to boarding schools where boys learned business and girls learned arts, sewing, and social manners.

Many middle-class families sent boys to learn a trade from a master. Boys as young as 9 years old left home to work as apprentices.

Savannah became a developed port town. Large wooden ships from England brought sugar and fabrics. They left the port with meat, lumber, rice, and indigo bound for England.

A blacksmith shows his apprentice how to shape metal into useful tools and other items, such as horseshoes.

Chapter 6:
The Slow Road to Revolution

As the American Colonies grew, so did their unhappiness with British leaders. The British Empire was in debt after defending the American Colonies in the French and Indian War (1754–1763). To raise money Parliament decided to tax the American colonists. In 1765 Parliament passed the Stamp Act, which required colonists to buy a stamp for all printed documents, such as newspapers. Colonists felt cheated because they did not have any say in the British government, especially in making such laws.

Split Loyalties

The Georgia Colony was divided. As a new royal colony, Georgia was slower than the other colonies to protest unfair taxes. The majority of Georgians felt loyal to England. They were known as **Loyalists**. Many of Georgia's older colonists grew up in England and still trusted their homeland.

Many American colonists protested the taxes that Britain placed on them.

Wealthy people were slow to protest too. They made their money by selling goods to England, so protesting would be bad for their businesses. Plus, Georgia's royal governor James Wright was very popular. The Loyalists did not want to remove him from power. As a result Georgia was the only colony that actually sold the stamps.

Most frontier farmers eventually supported America's independence. They did not benefit much from British rule and saw opportunity in a new nation. They wanted democracy, a government run by the people, not a king. In 1776 Governor Wright was arrested by **Patriots** and soon fled to the British.

The First Continental Congress met at Carpenter's Hall in Philadelphia. Georgia was the only colony that didn't attend.

A series of taxation laws called the Townshend Acts in 1767 further stirred up trouble. This time Georgia's Commons House of Assembly, its governing body, sent a request to King George III asking him to remove the taxes. A group of Georgian Patriots wrote eight resolutions criticizing the king and Parliament.

Patriot leaders tried to unite the colonies against King George III. They organized a Continental Congress in Philadelphia, Pennsylvania. The leaders wanted representatives from all 13 Colonies to meet to discuss and make decisions together. However, Georgia's leaders did not send any representatives to the First Continental Congress.

Loyalist—a colonist who was loyal to Great Britain during the Revolutionary War

Patriot—a person who sided with the colonies during the Revolutionary War

Fighting for Independence

Relations with England did not improve. In 1775 the Americans and British exchanged gunfire during small battles in Lexington and Concord, Massachusetts. The conflict started the Revolutionary War. America called its army the Continental army, and it wanted Georgia on its side. When Georgia's government remained undecided, the 12 other colonies stopped doing business with the colony. This **boycott** changed the minds of Georgia's leaders. Citizens had to choose sides, and many Loyalists fled the Georgia Colony, moving south to Florida or the West Indies.

In Colonial times people would pour hot tar over criminals and then stick feathers to them as a form of punishment. Here, Patriots tar and feather a Loyalist. Such cruel treatment forced many Loyalists out of Georgia.

"... all, gentle and simple, were made to declare whether they were on the side of the King or for the ... rebels. If a Tory [Loyalist] refused to join the people, he was imprisoned, and tarred and feathered ... All of the public officers under Government remained loyal and quit the country ..."

—Elizabeth Lichtenstein Johnston, a Georgia Loyalist

Georgia

The Georgia Colony sent five representatives when the Second Continental Congress met in 1775. There, all 13 Colonies agreed to band together as a nation independent from Great Britain. The Continental Congress also decided that each colony should write its own constitution. In July 1776 Button Gwinnett, Lyman Hall, and George Walton of Georgia approved the Declaration of Independence. A Patriot doctor named Noble Jones helped write Georgia's constitution, which was **ratified** on February 5, 1777.

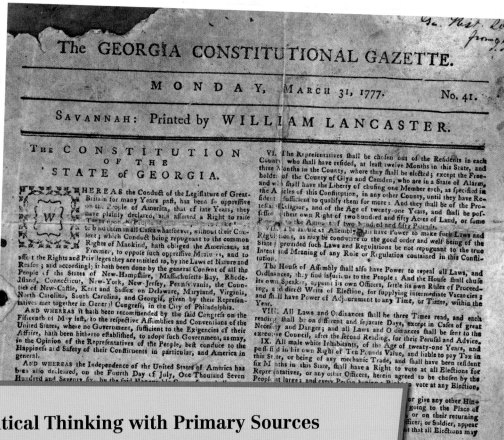

Critical Thinking with Primary Sources

The Georgia Constitution was published in a newspaper called *The Georgia Constitutional Gazette*. What date was it published? If it were published today, what other ways might journalists use to share it with Georgia's people?

boycott—to stop buying something to show support for an idea or group
ratify—to formally approve

Savannah Seized

The American Colonies were at war with Britain, but Georgia could not offer very many soldiers to the Continental army. Because of its small population, Georgia could barely defend itself. On December 29, 1778, with only about 700 soldiers defending Savannah, a British force of more than 2,000 soldiers attacked the city. At that time in the war, the British plan was to move troops to the South. They wanted to take back Georgia, and then take South Carolina, all with the help of southern Loyalists. The British easily captured Savannah, and James Wright became governor again.

The British Army then took Augusta, Georgia, and from there sent out officers to raise Loyalist **militia** troops from the countryside.

British troops storm the city of Savannah in 1778 while the town's residents try desperately to defend themselves.

Did You Know?

Georgia had the smallest population of the Southern Colonies when the Revolutionary War began. Historians estimate there were only about 50,000 colonists and slaves in the colony.

On February 14, 1779, about 600 new Loyalist troops were on their way to join the British in Augusta. They stopped to rest at Kettle Creek, near present-day Washington, Georgia. A small force of 340 Patriots surprised them and overran their camp. The Loyalist leader was shot and killed. Although the Patriots were outnumbered, the Loyalists fled, and only a few escaped to the British Army. Encouraged by the victory at the Battle of Kettle Creek, an army of 5,000 American, French, and French colonial troops from the Caribbean tried to recapture Savannah later in 1779. But the Americans were defeated, and the British would hold Savannah until nearly the end of the war.

During this unsettled time, an estimated 5,000 slaves escaped from Georgia. Others tried to fight for their freedom. British troops promised enslaved men freedom in exchange for joining the British Army.

American forces tried to take back the city of Savannah in 1779. But even with help from French troops, the Patriots lost many more soldiers and the British continued to hold Savannah.

militia—a group of volunteer citizens who are organized to fight but are not professional soldiers

Fighting in the Uplands

Although Britain had control over the coastal area around Savannah, fighting continued in the Uplands region. Patriots and Loyalists in the Uplands created their own militias. The militias burned each other's homes, ambushed each other on the roads, and murdered each other's families.

The Continental army sent troops to Georgia in the summer of 1781 to help the Patriot militia control the Uplands. British troops continued to occupy Savannah until July 1782. When they left James Wright lost his political power. He too fled Georgia and sailed back to England.

A French map from 1779 shows the Siege of Savannah by the American forces. However, the siege failed, and the British controlled the city until 1782.

Nancy Hart (1735?–1830)

Nancy Hart was a tough frontier Patriot born around 1735. During the War for Independence, she and her brave daughter Sukey fought for the Patriots. According to legend, in 1780 five or six Loyalists arrived at Nancy's cabin demanding food. Sukey pretended to go out to the well for water but ran to the nearest Patriot home instead. When the soldiers put down their guns to relax, Nancy took one of the guns and threatened to shoot the men. A soldier lunged at her, and she shot him. The other soldiers didn't dare try to escape. Sukey came back with more Patriots, who hanged the Tories. Nancy became the first woman in America to have a county named for her, Hart County, Georgia. True or not Nancy's story is an example of how ordinary citizens did brave and heroic things during the War for Independence.

Chapter 7:
From Colony to State

The years between the Revolutionary War and the ratification of the U.S. Constitution (1782–1788) were chaotic times of change for Georgia. Rich Loyalists and enslaved people fled. The Upland Patriots stayed in Georgia and claimed more power in the state's local, democratic governments. They started public schools and established the University of Georgia.

The University of Georgia was created by the state government in 1785, as its seal shows. But the first permanent university building wasn't built until 1806.

Did You Know?

One of the first things the new Georgia government decided to do was give western land to its war veterans. Although this land belonged to the Creeks, they were often forced off it. Relations between the Creeks and Americans worsened after the Revolutionary War. In the early 1800s, the Creeks fought battles for their Georgia land but were forced to give up much of it.

Noble W. Jones (1720?–1805)

Noble Jones was born in England and traveled as a boy to the Georgia Colony on the *Ann* in 1733. His political career began in 1755 when he served in Georgia's Commons House. During the Revolutionary War, Jones became a rebellious Patriot leader. Governor James Wright felt threatened by Jones' anti-British views.

The shots exchanged in 1775 at Lexington and Concord charged Jones' political career. He wrote Georgia's Colonial constitution in 1777 and helped to start its new government. As a founding father of Georgia, Jones was nicknamed the "Morning Star of Liberty."

Jones fled Savannah when the British captured the city in 1778. But British troops caught him in South Carolina and put him in a Florida prison. As soon as he was released, he went to Philadelphia, where he represented Georgia at the Second Continental Congress. Jones outlived all of the other original Georgia colonists. He had played a part in the history of the Georgia Colony from its beginning with the voyage of the *Ann*. And he also saw it through to its end during the fight to make it an independent state.

Defining a New Nation

From Georgia four representatives went to the Constitutional Convention in Philadelphia in 1787. At the meeting representatives from the former colonies discussed how to form a national government. They disagreed about the role of government, but in the end, they wrote the U.S. Constitution.

Back in Georgia a group of men debated whether or not to accept the Constitution. They understood that slavery was important for their economy. They worried that a strong central government would deny them the right to hold slaves. On the other hand, they knew they needed a strong central government for protection because the Creeks and Spanish threatened their safety.

George Washington (standing on right) watches as representatives from the 13 Colonies sign the U.S. Constitution.

They decided to join the other states in the hope of gaining their protection. On January 2, 1788, Georgia became the fourth state to ratify the Constitution.

Georgia began as a dream to help England's poor. Although that dream was never made real, Georgia still grew to become an independent state.

ABRAHAM BALDWIN.
Nat-1754 — Ob-1807.

WILLIAM FEW.
Nat-1748 — Ob-1828.

Representatives Abraham Baldwin (left) and William Few (right) signed the U.S. Constitution for Georgia.

Timeline

1540 Looking for gold Spanish explorer Hernando de Soto enters present-day Georgia from Spanish-occupied Florida.

1565 Pedro Menendez de Aviles claims land in Florida and later in Georgia for Spain.

1728 Chief Tomochichi and his Yamacraw followers settle on bluffs above the Savannah River.

1730 Georgia's board of trustees writes the Oglethorpe Plan, a proposal for a new colony.

1732 King George II signs a royal charter that approves the Georgia Colony.

1733 The ship *Ann* arrives in America with James Oglethorpe and the first group of Georgian colonists.

1734 Oglethorpe, Tomochichi, and several other Yamacraws sail to England.

1739 Britain declares war on Spain, marking the start of the War of Jenkins' Ear.

1742 Oglethorpe stops a Spanish invasion at the Battle of Bloody Marsh.

1751 Slavery becomes legal in Georgia.

1752 Georgia becomes a royal colony.

1754 The French and Indian War begins. When the war ends in 1763, the British government is left in debt.

1761 James Wright becomes the royal governor of Georgia.

1765 Great Britain imposes the Stamp Act.

1767 Great Britain imposes the Townshend Acts, which place taxes on tea, glass, paper, and paint.

1774 Delegates from 12 colonies meet at the First Continental Congress to discuss Great Britain's unfair laws. Georgia does not participate.

1775 In April American militiamen and British troops clash at the Battles of Lexington and Concord in Massachusetts. This marks the beginning of the Revolutionary War.

1776 Georgia delegates attending the Second Continental Congress sign the Declaration of Independence.

1777 Georgia's Colonial government writes and ratifies its first constitution.

1778 British troops capture Savannah.

1780 Nancy Hart stands up to Loyalist soldiers on the Georgia frontier.

1781 The British surrender to General George Washington in October after the Battle of Yorktown in Virginia.

1782 British troops and former Governor James Wright leave Savannah.

1783 Great Britain officially recognizes the United States as an independent nation with the signing of the Treaty of Paris.

1787 Four delegates from Georgia attend the Constitutional Convention and help draft the U.S. Constitution.

1788 Georgia becomes the fourth state to ratify the U.S. Constitution.

Glossary

alliance (uh-LY-uhnts)—an agreement between groups to work together

banish (BAN-ish)—to force someone to leave a country as a punishment

boycott (BOY-kot)—to stop buying something to show support for an idea or group

charter (CHAR-tuhr)—an official document granting permission to set up a new colony, organization, or company

colony (KAH-luh-nee)—a place that is settled by people from another country and is controlled by that country

confederacy (kunh-FED-ur-uh-see)—a union of people or groups with a common goal

debtor (DET-uhr)—someone who owes money to another person or organization

diplomat (DIP-luh-mat)—someone who deals with other nations to create or maintain good relationships

guerrilla warfare (guh-RIL-uh WOR-fair)—a battle strategy using small groups of fighters to carry out surprise attacks against enemy forces

immigrant (IM-uh-gruhnt)—someone who comes from one country to live permanently in another country

indentured servant (in-DEN-churd SUR-vuhnt)—a person who works for someone else for a certain period of time in return for payment of travel and living costs

indigo (IN-duh-goh)—a plant that produces a deep-blue dye

Loyalist (LOI-uh-list)—a colonist who was loyal to Great Britain during the Revolutionary War

militia (muh-LISH-uh)—a group of volunteer citizens who are organized to fight but are not professional soldiers

mission (MISH-uhn)—a church or other place where people from a religious group live and work trying to spread their faith

Parliament (PAHR-luh-muhnt)—Great Britain's lawmaking body

Patriot (PAY-tree-uht)—a person who sided with the colonies during the Revolutionary War

Protestant (PROT-uh-stuhnt)—a Christian who does not belong to the Roman Catholic or the Orthodox Church

ratify (RAT-uh-fye)—to formally approve

royal colony (ROI-uhl KAH-luh-nee)—a colony controlled by a monarch or his representatives

seamstress (SEEM-struhss)—a woman who sews for a living

smuggler (SMUHG-lur)—a person who sneaks illegal goods into or out of a country

trustee (TRUHSS-tee)—a person who has been given responsibility for someone else's property

Critical Thinking Using the Common Core

1. In what ways did the Oglethorpe Plan succeed? In what ways did it fail? (Key Ideas and Details)

2. Imagine you are a middle-class silversmith living in Colonial Savannah. If you join the Patriots, you will not be able to purchase silver and tools from England anymore. If you join the Loyalists, you may get attacked by the Continental army. What do you do? Explain your choice. (Integration of Knowledge and Ideas)

3. You decide to turn this book *Exploring the Georgia Colony* into a play. Who would you cast as the main characters? Why? (Craft and Structure)

Read More

Asselin, Kristine Carlson. *The Real Story About Government and Politics in Colonial America*. Life in the American Colonies. Mankato, Minn.: Capstone Press, 2012.

Cunningham, Kevin. *The Georgia Colony*. A True Book. New York: Children's Press, 2012.

Machajewski, Sarah. *The Colony of Georgia*. Spotlight on the 13 Colonies. New York: PowerKids Press, 2015.

Winter, Jonah. *The Founding Fathers! Those Horse Ridin', Fiddle-Playin', Book-Readin', Gun-Totin' Gentlemen Who Started America*. New York: Atheneum Books for Young Readers, 2015.

Internet Sites

FactHound offers a safe, fun way to find Internet sites related to this book. All of the sites on FactHound have been researched by our staff.
Here's all you do:
Visit *www.facthound.com*
Type in this code: 9781515722410

 Check out projects, games and lots more at
www.capstonekids.com

Source Notes

Page 11, callout quote: The Gentleman of Elvas. "The Narrative of the Expedition of Hernando de Soto." *Georgia Voices: A Documentary History to 1872*, by Spencer Bidwell King, Jr. Athens, Ga.: University of Georgia Press, 2010, p. 1.

Page 17, callout quote: "Charter of Georgia: 1732." *The Avalon Project: Lillian Goldman Law Library*. Accessed May 19, 2016. http://avalon.law.yale.edu/18th_century/ga01.asp.

Page 32, callout quote: Elizabeth Lichtenstein Johnston. *Recollections of a Georgia Loyalist*. New York: Bankside Press, 1901, 44–45. Accessed April 19, 2016. https://archive.org/stream/recollectionsofg00john.

Regions of the 13 Colonies		
Northern Colonies	**Middle Colonies**	**Southern Colonies**
Connecticut, Massachusetts, New Hampshire, Rhode Island	Delaware, New Jersey, New York, Pennsylvania	Georgia, Maryland, North Carolina, South Carolina, Virginia
land more suitable for hunting than farming; trees cut down for lumber; trapped wild animals for their meat and fur; fished in rivers, lakes, and ocean	the "Breadbasket" colonies—rich farmland, perfect for growing wheat, corn, rye, and other grains	soil better for growing tobacco, rice, and indigo; crops grown on huge farms called plantations; landowners depended heavily on servants and slaves to work in the fields

Select Bibliography

"Colonial Era 1733–1775." Digital Library of Georgia: Georgia's History and Culture Online. Accessed April 19, 2016. http://dlg.galileo.usg.edu/TimePeriods/ColonialEra.html.

De Brahm, John Gerar William. *A Map of the Indian Nations in the Southern Department*. Hargrett Rare Book and Manuscript Library Rare Map Collection. Drawing. 1766. Accessed April 19, 2016. http://hmap.libs.uga.edu/hmap/view?docId=hmap/hmap1766d4.xml;query=;brand=default.

GeorgiaInfo: An Online Georgia Almanac. Accessed on April 19, 2016. http://georgiainfo.galileo.usg.edu/topics/history.

Grimes, John. "Eulogy on the Life and Character of Dr. Noble Wymberley Jones." *The Georgia Historical Quarterly* 4, no. 4 (1920): Georgia Historical Society: 141–158.

Hahn, Steven C. *The Life and Times of Mary Musgrove*. Gainesville, Fla.: University Press of Florida, 2012.

Jones, George. *His Majesty's Colony of Georgia in America*. Hargrett Rare Book and Manuscript Library Rare Map Collection. Drawing. 1734. Accessed April 19, 2016. http://hmap.libs.uga.edu/hmap/view?docId=hmap/hmap1734g6b.xml;query=;brand=default

Juricek, John, *Colonial Georgia and the Creeks*. Gainesvill, Fla.: University Press of Florida, 2010.

King, Spencer Bidwell, Jr. *Georgia Voices: A Documentary History to 1872*. Athens, Ga.: University of Georgia Press, 2010.

Lancaster, William. *Georgia Constitution 1777*. Georgia Historical Society: Digital Image Catalogue. Accessed May 19, 2016. http://georgiahistory.pastperfect-online.com/37659cgi/mweb.exe?request=record;id=BF330178-A838-4848-93F7-700288752883;type=301.

Lockley, Timothy J. "Slavery in Revolutionary Georgia." New Georgia Encyclopedia. Accessed April 19, 2016. http://www.georgiaencyclopedia.org/articles/history-archaeology/slavery-revolutionary-georgia.

The Most Delightful Country of the Universe: Promotional Literature of the Colony of Georgia, 1717-1734. Foreward by Trevor R. Reese. Savannah, Ga.: Beehive Press, 1972.

Wood, Betty. "Slavery in Colonial Georgia." New Georgia Encyclopedia. Accessed April 19, 2016. http://www.georgiaencyclopedia.org/articles/history-archaeology/slavery-colonial-georgia.

Index